Mysterious People

A CHAPTER BOOK

BY MICHELE SOBEL SPIRN

children's press®

A Division of Scholastic Inc.
New York   Toronto   London   Auckland   Sydney
Mexico City   New Delhi   Hong Kong
Danbury, Connecticut

For Steve, Josh, and Kirsten

ACKNOWLEDGMENTS

The author and publisher would like to thank all those who gave
their time and knowledge to help with this book. In particular, special
thanks go to Joann Fletcher and Dr. Orin Starn, Professor of Cultural
Anthropology, Duke University.

Library of Congress Cataloging-in-Publication Data

Spirn, Michele.
  Mysterious people : a chapter book / by Michele Sobel Spirn.
    p. cm. — (True tales)
Includes bibliographical references and index.
  ISBN 0-516-25181-3 (lib. bdg.)   0-516-25454-5 (pbk.)
  1. Biography—Juvenile literature. 2. Nefertiti, Queen of Egypt, 14th cent.
B.C.—Juvenile literature. 3. Hauser, Kaspar, 1812-1833—Juvenile literature.
4. Ishi, d. 1916—Juvenile literature. 5. Otzi (Ice mummy)—Juvenile
literature. 6. Curiosities and wonders—Juvenile literature. I. Title. II. Series.

CT105.S725 2005
920.02—dc22

2005004782

1 2 3 4 5 6 7 8 9 10 R 14 13 12 11 10 09 08 07 06 05

CONTENTS

INTRODUCTION

Most of us like to read mysteries or watch them on TV or in the movies. We like to try to figure out the answers to these mysteries. In this book, you'll read about mysteries that really happened. You'll find that we still don't know everything about these mysterious people.

Queen Nefertiti helped rule Egypt for fourteen years. Then, one day, she disappeared. Kaspar Hauser, a teenage boy, mysteriously appeared in a German town. Who was he? Ishi was the last member of a Native-American tribe. He kept many of his people's secrets, including his real name. No one knows for sure what happened to Ötzi, a man who lived more than 5,000 years ago. His mummy was found frozen on a mountain in the Alps.

Read about these mysterious people. See what you think. Maybe you can come up with your own ideas about these people of mystery.

CHAPTER ONE

THE BEAUTY QUEEN

Joann Fletcher walked into the dark **tomb** (TOOM). She saw three **mummies** in front of her. They were not wrapped, like most mummies. One had a shaved head. Near the mummy was a wig of short hair. It was the kind of wig **royal** women of Egypt had worn.

Joann looked at the woman's body. Someone had cut her mouth. Her right arm had been torn off. Somebody had tried to smash her feet. Who was this woman? Why had people tried to hurt her after she was dead?

Joann Fletcher

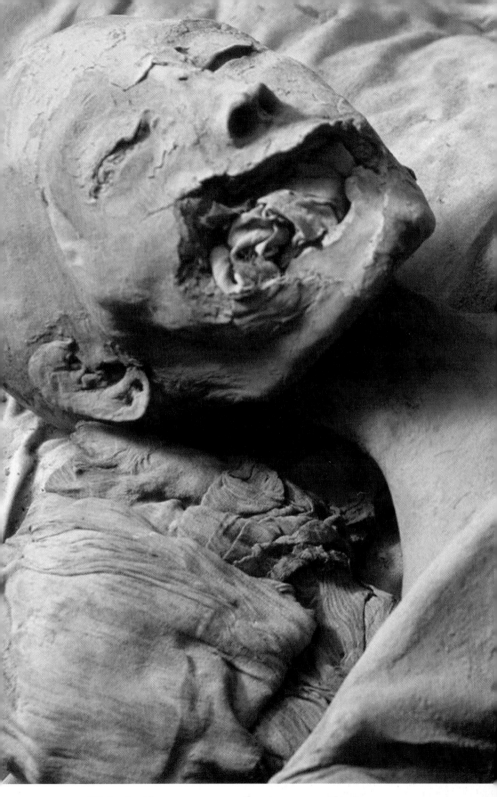

This is the mummy of a woman that Joann Fletcher found.

This sculpture of Nefertiti
shows her great beauty.

After twelve years of studying this mummy, Joann believes it was one of the most famous women of all time. She thinks this mummy is what is left of the mysterious Queen Nefertiti of **ancient** (AYN-shunt) Egypt.

Who was Nefertiti? Everyone agrees that she was beautiful. In fact, her name means "the beautiful woman has come." There is no mystery about her looks. There is plenty of mystery about her life.

Queen Nefertiti lived in Egypt more than three thousand years ago. She married Akhenaten, a **pharaoh** (FAIR-oh), or king, of Egypt. Akhenaten and Nefertiti began ruling Egypt together in 1352 B.C. Many carvings show them kissing. They are also shown playing with their six children, all girls.

The most important thing Nefertiti and Akhenaten did together was start a new religion. The people of Egypt had worshipped many gods for thousands of years. Akhenaten decided that the sun god

A sculpture of King Akhenaten

Aten was the only god his people should worship. He got rid of all the other gods.

At that time, a lot of people made money from the worship of many gods. There were thousands of **priests** who were paid to take care of the gods. Workers were paid to build hundreds of **temples**. Artists made and sold **images** of the gods. People believed if the gods were happy, Egypt would be a safe, rich place to live.

They also thought the gods were important in the **afterlife.** This was the life people believed they would have after they died. Egyptians were buried with food and their favorite things. This was so they could have a good time after they died. A happy

This scene from the Egyptian *Book of the Dead* shows someone entering the afterlife.

In ancient Egypt, temples were built as homes for the gods.

afterlife was certain if the living person had pleased the gods.

Akhenaten believed his god was the best. He built a temple to Aten and closed other temples. He sent his men to destroy the statues of other gods.

The people of Egypt worried. What would happen when they died? The priests whose temples Akhenaten had destroyed were angry.

Akhenaten did not care. He was happy with his new god. Six years after Akhenaten became pharaoh, he and Nefertiti left the capital of Thebes to build a city for his new religion. Today this spot is called Tel el Amarna. Akhenaten built big palaces and a temple to Aten.

In this sculpture, the sun shines on Akhenaten, Nefertiti, and two of their daughters.

Akhenaten made Nefertiti a priest of Aten. He had her image carved onto the four corners of his **coffin**. Usually, such carvings were of female gods.

Then, thirteen years after Akhenaten took the throne, Nefertiti disappeared. Her name does not appear in Egyptian writings after that. There were no more images of her. What happened?

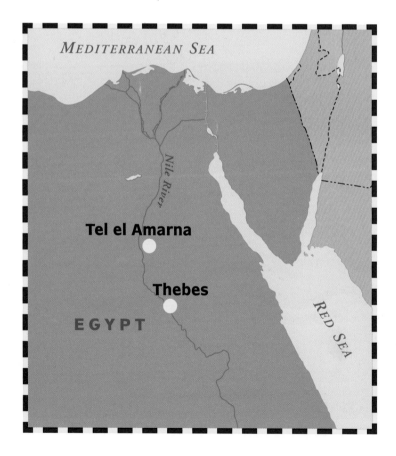

The inside of an Egyptian tomb

Some people who have studied ancient Egypt believe she died. Others think she retired. Joann Fletcher believes she may have been killed. "It's quite possible," says Joann, "that Nefertiti may have tried to become pharaoh with Akhenaten. Perhaps the priests killed her because they did not want her to have more power."

Akhenaten died seventeen years after he became pharaoh. After his death, his followers returned to Thebes and their old gods. The priests took Akhenaten's name off his statues. They destroyed his temples. No one wanted to remember Akhenaten or Nefertiti.

Joann Fletcher believes the priests hated Nefertiti. She thinks they hated her because she helped Akhenaten destroy the old gods. Did the priests try to stop her from having an afterlife? Egyptians of that time believed that hurting a mummy could stop it from living again. Nefertiti could not breathe if they smashed her mouth. If her feet were hurt, she could not walk into the afterlife.

Could this explain the condition of the mummy? Is the mummy really even Nefertiti? No one knows for sure. Nefertiti and her life and her death are still a mystery.

**Joann Fletcher with the mummy she believes
is Queen Nefertiti**

CHAPTER TWO

PRINCE OF MYSTERY

On May 28, 1828, a teenage boy was found in Nuremberg, Germany. He **staggered** through the streets as if he were drunk. When a man came up to him, the boy held out a letter. It was addressed to a **captain**. The man took the boy to the captain's house.

Servants gave the boy some meat, but he spat it out. He wanted only bread and water. The boy cried and pointed to his feet. When he spoke, no one could understand him. Finally, he fell asleep.

The city of Nuremberg, Germany, in the 1800s

When the captain came home, he read the letter the boy carried. The person who had written the letter said that he could no longer care for the boy. He suggested the boy be trained as a soldier. The letter was not signed.

The captain took the boy to the police. The police gave him a pen, ink, and paper and asked him to write. They were surprised when he wrote his name: "Kaspar Hauser."

A local family agreed to care for Kaspar. One of the sons taught Kaspar how to talk. Kaspar told the family about his past life. He said he had been locked up in a small cage. His jailer had given him bread and water.

One day, his jailer gave him some books. He told Kaspar he must learn to read and write. He said Kaspar's father was a soldier who rode on a horse. Soon after that, the man came to take Kaspar away. He said that he was taking Kaspar to his father so that Kaspar could become a rider like his father. When they got close to Nuremberg, the man told Kaspar to go on alone.

In July 1828, Kaspar went to live with Professor Daumer, a university professor. Daumer helped Kaspar get used to the world. Kaspar learned to write letters. He rode for hours on horseback. He was able to eat regular food.

An artist's drawing of Kaspar Hauser

One day, when Kaspar was home alone, a man attacked him with a knife. Kaspar was not badly hurt. He believed that the man who had stabbed him was the jailer who had kept him locked up as a child.

The police tried to find his attacker, but they failed. It was whispered that Kaspar was part of a royal German family, the Badens. People said he looked like members of the family. It was said that the Grand Duke of Baden had wanted Kaspar killed. Some people wondered if he had ordered the attack on Kaspar.

For his own safety, Kaspar was sent to live with another family. Two policemen guarded him. An English lord named Philip Henry Stanhope became friends with Kaspar. In 1831, Lord Stanhope took Kaspar away from the friends he knew. He took Kaspar to a town called Ansbach.

These two statues of Kaspar Hauser are in Ansbach. The one in front shows him when he was first discovered. The one in back shows him a few years later.

On December 14, 1831, Kaspar went to a park in Ansbach. A man was waiting for him. He said he had news about Kaspar's mother. As Kaspar came closer, the man pulled out a knife and stabbed Kaspar.

Kaspar died from the stabbing on December 17, 1831. He was twenty-one years old. His gravestone reads: "Here lies Kaspar Hauser, riddle of his time. His birth was unknown, his death mysterious."

In 2002, however, his birth became less mysterious. Testing was done on Kaspar's **DNA**. His DNA was compared to the DNA of a living member of the royal House of Baden. The results showed that Kaspar may indeed have been a Baden. The poor prince of mystery had probably been kidnapped as a very young child.

Had someone within the Baden family wanted to get rid of the little boy? Was Kaspar kidnapped as a child and then later killed so that someone else could become a prince of Baden instead of him? No one knows for sure.

The words on Kaspar Hauser's gravestone
are written in Latin.

CHAPTER THREE

THE LAST YAHI

On August 28, 1911, Ishi came out of the hills near Oroville, California. He was starving. He wore little clothing. For the past forty years, he had been living with his tribe, the Yahi. Now they were all dead. He was the last Yahi.

The Yahi people had lived and hunted in California in peace. Then, in 1849, gold was found in the state. Many of the native people were killed by **pioneers** coming west for the gold. The new people took over the land on which the Yahi had lived and hunted. They killed the deer the

Ishi soon after he arrived in Oroville

For many years, Ishi lived with his people in the hills near Oroville, California. This is how the area looks today.

Many people headed to California when gold
was discovered there in 1848.

The Yahi stole the settlers' cattle in order to survive.

Yahi needed for food. The Yahi had nothing to eat. So they stole the settlers' cattle and horses. The settlers then hunted and killed the Yahi. Other Yahi died from diseases that the settlers brought with them. These were diseases the natives had never seen or had before.

People think Ishi was born after the gold rush. His father had been killed in 1865 along with many other Yahi. By the time Ishi was an adult, there were less than forty people in his tribe.

In 1908, a group of men working for the power company found the hidden camp of Ishi and his family. Ishi was away. There were four people in the camp. When the men came, three of the people ran away. They left Ishi's mother. She was old, sick, and could not walk. The men did not hurt Ishi's mother. They did, however, take away all of the Yahi's blankets, food, and tools. After Ishi returned, his mother died.

For three years, Ishi tried to live on his own. Finally, he gave up and left the hills. When he reached the town of Oroville, the sheriff put him in jail to protect him. Other Native Americans were brought in to try to talk with Ishi. He did not understand them. No one knew what tribe he belonged to.

Finally, two men who studied ancient people heard about Ishi. Alfred Kroeber and Thomas Waterman were professors at the University of California. They wanted to write down the histories of Native American tribes before they died out. They made friends with Ishi. They were the ones who gave him the name "Ishi." Ishi never told anyone his true name. In his tribe, it was **forbidden** to tell one's name to strangers.

Ishi's name means "man" in Yahi.

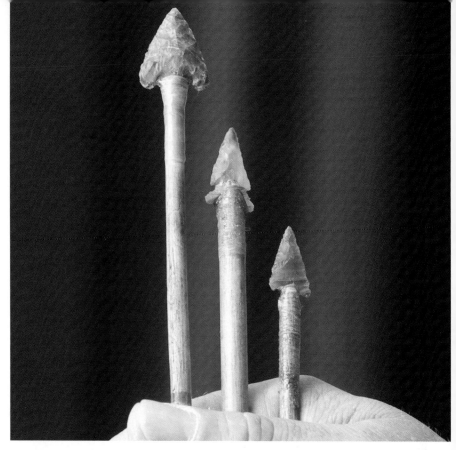
The Yahi made arrowheads like the ones shown above.

For four years and seven months, Ishi taught the two professors about his tribe. They learned the Yahi language. Ishi was happy to talk with people. He showed them how he made **arrowheads**, bows, and spears for hunting. He recorded Yahi songs, stories, and history. In 1914, the professors even went on a trip with Ishi to his old camp. At first, Ishi did not want to go. He was afraid to go back to a place where he had been so sad. Finally, he said yes. The professors marked places where Ishi had lived and hunted. They made maps of where the Yahi had been. They learned much about the Yahi way of life.

Alfred Kroeber with Ishi

In 1916, Ishi died from **tuberculosis** (tu-bur-kyuh-LOH-siss), a lung disease. Thomas Waterman said, "He was my best friend." A doctor who had become Ishi's friend wrote, "He was kind; he had courage … and though all had been taken from him, there was no bitterness in his heart."

An urn containing Ishi's ashes

This mask was made of Ishi's face after Ishi's death.
When he died, so did the last of the Yahi.

CHAPTER FOUR

THE ICEMAN

On September 19, 1991, a man and his wife were hiking in the Ötztal Alps. These mountains lie between Austria and Italy. The couple were enjoying themselves when they got a big surprise. There, in the ice, was a dead body. Who was it?

The police were told about the body. They tried to pull it out of the ice by its clothes. They tore the clothes badly. They drilled into the ice, making a hole in the body's hip. When they forced the body into a coffin, they broke its left arm. They made many mistakes. How were they to know that the body, a man, had died over 5,300 years ago?

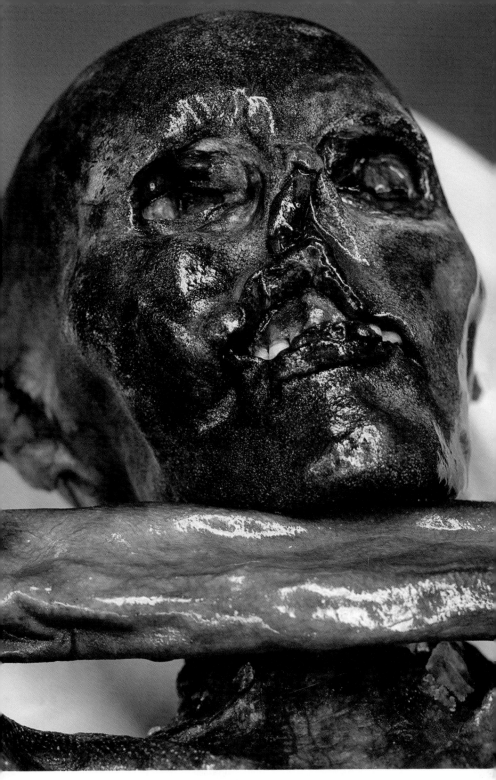

The body above was found frozen
on a mountain in the Alps.

Scientists named the dead man Ötzi the Iceman after the mountains where he was found. He is one of the oldest and best-preserved mummies ever found.

At first, scientists who studied Ötzi thought he got caught in a snowstorm. They believed he fell asleep and froze to death. Then they found an arrowhead in his left shoulder. They also discovered he had a bad **wound** in one hand. Had he been in a fight? What had happened to Ötzi?

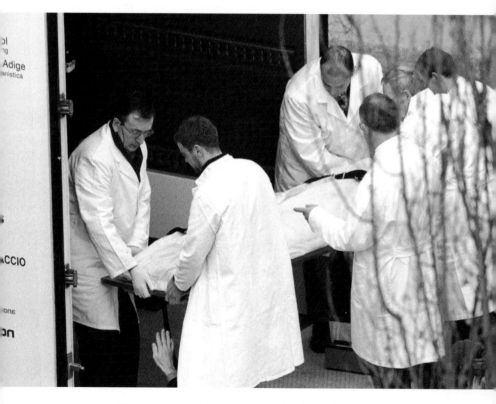

These workers are bringing Ötzi to a lab.

Some of Ötzi's belongings

Scientists have many ideas. Some think a hunter shot Ötzi by accident and then buried him. Others believe that Ötzi was a **shepherd**. Maybe he was killed by someone who wanted his sheep. Maybe a robber wanted his copper ax. One professor thinks that Ötzi fought a robber. Then he hid in the deep snow. While Ötzi waited for the robber to leave, he fell asleep and died.

Those who have studied Ötzi have learned more about where he lived. They think he lived his whole life within 40 miles (64 kilometers) of where he met his death. They know he was between twenty-five and forty years old. Ötzi was short. He was only about 63 inches (160 centimeters) tall.

He had **tattoos** (ta-TOOZ) on his body. Scientists do not think the tattoos were for decoration. They think that Ötzi believed the tattoos would help heal certain aches and pains he may have had. He wore a coat made out of grass, a bearskin hat, and good snowshoes. He had **flints** for making a fire. Ötzi also carried lots of **moss**. Scientists think he may have used the moss for medicine.

Ötzi being examined by scientists

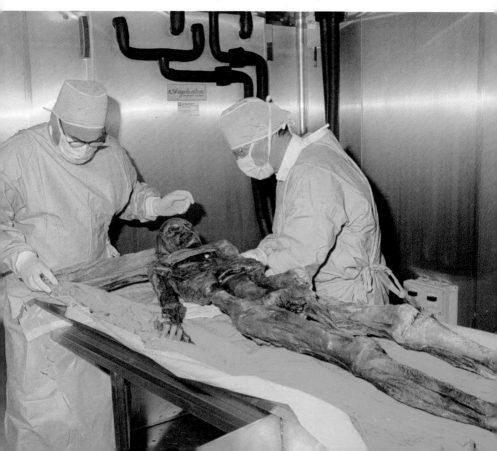

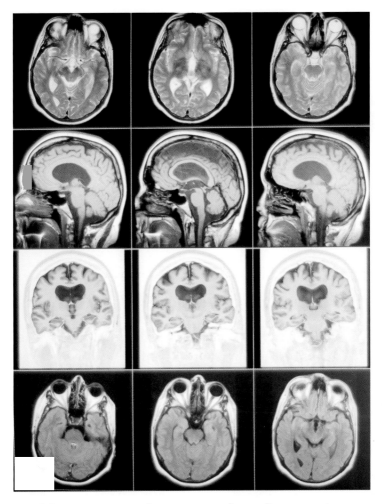

This CAT scan shows a series of computer images of a human brain.

How do scientists know so much about Ötzi? They discovered his age and how long ago he had died by doing tests on his bones. They found out more about him by doing a **CAT scan** on him. This is a test doctors use to see inside a person's body. Ötzi's CAT scan showed a lump of food inside him. It was his last meal. He had eaten it eight hours before he died. What had Ötzi eaten? His last food was a piece of hard bread made out of wheat, some greens or vegetables, and a piece of meat. He was also carrying some berries for a snack.

Scientists continue to study Ötzi. He is the best example of how people lived during the late **Stone Age**. Ötzi's body now lies in a museum in Italy. There people will continue to study and learn about Ötzi and the life he led thousands of years ago. The only thing they will never know for sure is how this iceman of mystery died.

A scientist used the shape of Ötzi's skull to make a model of what the Iceman might have looked like.

GLOSSARY

afterlife where people believe they will go after they die

ancient (AYN-shunt) from a long time ago; very old

arrowhead the sharp tip of an arrow

captain an officer who leads soldiers in an army

CAT scan a series of X rays that show the human body in slices

coffin a box used to bury a dead person

DNA a long chain of information that fits inside the cells of all living things; people who are related to each other have similarities in their DNA

flint a hard stone that makes sparks when struck with steel

forbidden not allowed

image a likeness of something, such as a drawing or statue

moss a rootless green plant that grows on damp soil, rocks, and tree trunks

mummy the body of a dead person that has been dried and saved

pharaoh (FAIR-oh) an ancient Egyptian king

pioneer one of the first people to settle in a new area

priest a religious leader

royal having to do with a king or queen or a member of their family

shepherd a person whose job is to look after sheep

stagger to walk in an unsteady manner

Stone Age a time when very early humans used tools and weapons made from stone

tattoo (ta-TOO) a picture that has been printed on a person's skin

temple a building used as a home for a god

tomb (TOOM) an underground room for the dead

tuberculosis (tu-bur-kyuh-LOH-siss) a serious disease that affects the lungs

wound an injury to the skin

FIND OUT MORE

The Beauty Queen
www.dsc.discovery.com/convergence/nefertiti/nefertiti.html
Tour an Egyptian tomb and learn more about Joann
Fletcher's ideas.

The Prince of Mystery
www.kbs.cs.tu-
berlin.de/~jutta/me/notes/kaspar_hauser.html
Read more about Kaspar Hauser.

The Last Yahi
www.gilanet.com/amerabo/ishipage.htm
Look at more photos of Ishi and examine the kinds of tools
the Yahi used.

The Iceman
www.dsc.discovery.com/convergence/iceman/iceman.html
Learn how studying Ötzi's body has changed what scientists
know about the Stone Age.

More Books to Read

Ice Mummy: The Discovery of a 5,000 Year-Old Man by Cathy
East Dubowski, Random House Children's Books, 2003

Ishi: The Last of His People by David Petersen,
Children's Press, 1991

*Secrets of the Mummies: Uncovering the Bodies of Ancient
Egyptians* by Shelley Tanaka, Hyperion Books for Children,
2000

Wild Children: Growing Up Without Human Contact by
Elaine Landau, Franklin Watts, 1998

INDEX

PHOTO CREDITS

MEET THE AUTHOR

Michele Sobel Spirn has been writing since she won a state essay contest at the age of sixteen. She has written over forty books for children, both fiction and nonfiction. Michele particularly enjoys reading mysteries. She has written three mysteries for children about two sisters who travel to faraway places. She lives in Brooklyn, New York, with her husband and many, many books.